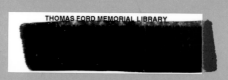

Wants Versus Needs

Possessions

Linda Staniford

heinemann raintree

© 2015 Heinamann Raintree
an imprint of Capstone Global Library, LLC
Chicago, Illinois

To contact Capstone Global Library, please call 800-747-4992, or visit our web site www.capstonepub.com

Edited by Linda Staniford and Shelly Lyons
Designed by Philippa Jenkins
Original illustrations © Capstone Global Library Ltd 2015
Picture research by Tracy Cummins
Production by Helen McCreath
Originated by Capstone Global Library Ltd
Printed and bound in China by Leo Paper Group

18 17 16 15 14
10 9 8 7 6 5 4 3 2 1

Library of Congress Cataloging-in-Publication Data
Staniford, Linda.
  Possessions / Linda Staniford.
    pages cm.—(Wants vs. needs)
  Includes bibliographical references and index.
  ISBN 978-1-4846-0945-3 (hb)—ISBN 978-1-4846-0950-7 (pb)—ISBN 978-1-4846-0960-6 (ebook) 1. Acquisitiveness—Juvenile literature. 2. Personal belongings—Juvenile literature. I. Title.

  BF698.35.A36.S73 2015
  155.3'32—dc23   2014015026

This book has been officially leveled by using the F&P Text Level Gradient™ Leveling System.

Acknowledgments
We would like to thank the following for permission to reproduce photographs: Alamy: © Kuttig, 20; Capstone Press: Philippa Jenkins, Cover Top, Design Elements; Getty Images: Andersen Ross, 13, 22 BL, Inti St Clair, 8, 23, Steve Debenport, 19, 23, Thomas Barwick, 12, 23, Vesnaandjic, 23; Shutterstock: Aprilphoto, 1, Cover Bottom, Goodluz, 4, Hurst Photo, 14, Mikhail Rulkov, 7, 22 TL, Back Cover, spotmatik, 15, Tyler Olson, 9, wavebreakmedia, 16, XiXinXing, 10, Zadorozhnyi Viktor, 6; Thinkstock: David Sacks, 21, Goodluz, 17, 22 BR, 23, Ingram Publishing, 5, LuminaStock, 18, monkeybusinessimages, 11, 22 TR.

Every effort has been made to contact copyright holders of material reproduced in this book. Any omissions will be rectified in subsequent printings if notice is given to the publisher.

Contents

What Are Needs and Wants?......................4

Do We Need Toys?..............................6

Do We Need Books?...........................8

How Do We Need to Travel?...............10

What Clothes Do We Need?..............12

What Do We Need in Our Homes?............14

Do We Need Computers?...................16

Do We Have Too Many Possessions?........18

Do We Need New Possessions?.................20

Quiz...22

Picture Glossary 23

Index.......................................24

Some words are shown in bold, **like this.** You can find them in the glossary on page 23.

What Are Needs and Wants?

Possessions are things we own. Some of our possessions are needs, like homes and clothes. We need them to live.

4

Some possessions are things we want but do not need. We like to have toys and computer games but we do not need them to live.

Do We Need Toys?

You need food to help you grow. You might need things to help you play. Do you need toys?

You may have been given lots of toys as gifts. It is nice to have new toys to play with. But do you really need them all?

Do We Need Books?

We need books to help us learn to read. Books also help us learn new **information**. It is good to own some books. You can read them whenever you want to.

You do not need to buy all your books. Instead, you can borrow books from the library.

How Do We Need to Travel?

Many families own a car. Some families need a car to get to work, school, and stores. Traveling by car is easy and fast.

You could walk or ride a bike for short trips. Walking and bike riding are good for you, too.

What Clothes Do We Need?

We need some clothes. They keep us warm or **protect** us from the sun. Sometimes we need special clothes for activities we might enjoy.

It is nice to have new clothes. It can be fun to wear different things. But you do not need lots of clothes.

What Do We Need in Our Homes?

Everyone needs somewhere to live. Your home gives you **shelter** and keeps you safe.

Every family needs different things in their home. Your friends may have things in their home that you do not have. Different families need different things.

Do We Need Computers?

Many families own a computer. Computer help us find important **information**. They also help us keep in touch with people and buy things we may need.

You may want other **electronics**, such as cell phones or tablets. You might want the latest computer game that your friend has. But do you need these things?

Do We Have Too Many Possessions?

Do you have more possessions than you need? Do you have things you do not want anymore? Maybe an adult can give them to people who need them.

Many children in the world do not have things they need. We can help them by **donating** clothes and other things they need.

Do We Need New Possessions?

It is okay to want new things sometimes. Old things can break or wear out. As you get older what you need changes.

It is important to think about what you already have and to decide if you really need it. You may want something but do you need it?

Quiz

Are these things needs or wants?

Picture Glossary

donate give to a charity

electronic operated by computer and machine parts

information knowledge or facts about something or someone

protect keep safe from danger or harm

shelter place where we feel safe

Index

bike riding 11

books 8–9

cars 10

cell phones 17

clothes 4, 12–13, 19

computer games 5, 17

computers 16–17

donating things 18–19

electronics 17, 23

homes 14–15

information 8, 16, 23

library 9

needs 4

new things 20

protect 12, 23

shelter 4, 14

tablets 17

toys 5, 6–7

travel 10–11

walking 11

wants 5

Note to Parents and Teachers

Reading nonfiction texts for information is an important part of a child's literary development. Readers can be encouraged to ask simple questions and then use the text to find the answers. Each chapter in this book begins with a question. Read the questions together. Look at the pictures. Talk about what the answer might be. Then, read the text to find out if your predictions were correct. To develop readers' inquiry skills, encourage them to think of other questions they might ask about the topic. Discuss where you could find the answers. Assist children in using the contents page, picture glossary, and index to practice research skills and new vocabulary words.